Alex Wheatle is one of the UK's most popular Black British authors. He has written books for adults and teenagers, including the critically acclaimed *Brixton Rock*, *Liccle Bit* and *Crongton Knights*. In 2008, he was awarded an MBE for services to literature and, in 2016, he won *The Guardian*'s children's fiction prize.

About Diffusion books

Diffusion publishes books for adults who are emerging readers. There are two series:

 Books in the Diamond series are ideally suited to those who are relatively new to reading or who have not practised their reading skills for some time (approximately Entry Level 2 to 3 in adult literacy levels).

 Books in the Star series are for those who are ready for the next step. These books will help to build confidence and inspire readers to tackle longer books (approximately Entry Level 3 to Level 1 in adult literacy levels).

Other books available in the Diamond series are:

Space Ark by Rob Childs

Snake by Matt Dickinson

Fans by Niall Griffiths

Breaking the Chain by Darren Richards

Lost at Sea by Joel Smith

Books available in the Star series are:

Not Such a Bargain by Toby Forward

Barcelona Away by Tom Palmer

Forty-six Quid and a Bag of Dirty Washing by Andy Croft

Bare Freedom by Andy Croft

One Shot by Lena Semaan

Nowhere to Run by Michael Crowley

Uprising
A true story

Alex Wheatle

diffusion

First published in Great Britain in 2017

Diffusion
an imprint of SPCK
36 Causton Street
London SW1P 4ST
www.spck.org.uk

ISBN 978-1-908713-10-0

Typeset by Lapiz Digital Services, Chennai
Printed in Great Britain by Severn, Gloucester
Subsequently digitally reprinted in Great Britain

Produced on paper from sustainable forests

Contents

Contents

1
Early life

My name is Alex Wheatle and I was born into scandal.

My mother was already married in Jamaica when she came to live in the UK. She had four daughters and one son. In 1961, she came to live in Brixton in London. She left behind in Jamaica her five children and her violent husband.

My father, also from Jamaica, was a single man. He had been in the UK since 1954.

He was also living in Brixton. He was a carpenter. He worked on the building sites of south London.

My parents met and had an affair. My mum became pregnant with me in the spring of 1962.

When my mother was six months pregnant, she had a surprise visitor. It was her husband. You can imagine the look on his face when my mother opened the door and he saw her big belly. There was no way he was going to let my mum look after me once I was born. In the early 1960s, women who had a child outside of marriage were scorned by their communities.

So, on a freezing cold January day, it was my father who picked me up from the hospital. He took me back to Brixton and put me in the care of his two sisters and different babysitters. I was three days old.

Soon afterwards Mum returned to Jamaica. I lost all touch with her.

When I was three years old, my father could not cope with me any more. He put me in the care of Lambeth social services. I was then sent to a children's home in the Surrey countryside.

Soon afterwards my father also went back to Jamaica.

I was abandoned.

The children's home was a sort of village. There were about eighty big houses with about twenty kids in each house. There were ten boys and ten girls. The houses were in the country and all you could see were fields, trees and bushes. It was nothing like Brixton.

My first memories are of scrubbing stone steps and filling buckets with coal for the lounge and dining-room fires. The staff at the home did not care that I had bad asthma. I still had to fill those buckets.

The staff also didn't know how to treat my skin or my hair. I ended up looking more grey than black. My afro looked like a chewed-up toffee apple!

I was beaten almost every day with whatever the staff had to hand – wooden hair brushes, belts, shoes and, once, with an iron fire poker. Then there were two times when a child psychiatrist sexually abused me. Man, he was there to help me and he did that to me.

I remember the mayor of Lambeth visiting us once. The staff put on a cricket match in his honour. They gave the mayor cups of tea and more cream cakes than he could eat. The children were not given any.

What do you think?

- What does Alex mean when he says, 'I was born into scandal'?

- Alex lived in what was called a 'care home'. In what ways is this a good or bad description of the place he grew up in?

- What do you think makes a real home?

2
Things fall apart

When I was in the children's home, I made friends with a mixed-race boy the same age as me. He was like me. He did not know any of his family. We were tight like brothers.

We slept with six other boys, in the same bedroom. One night, when I was ten, the bedroom door burst open. Three men walked in. They marched to where my friend was sleeping and they woke him up.

'Get up, get dressed and pack your bags. You're coming with us,' one of the men ordered.

'I'm not going,' said my friend.

'You're coming with us!' the man said again.

They began to drag him out of the room.

I asked the officer in charge where the men were taking my friend.

'You're not next of kin so you don't need to know,' he said.

'What's next of kin?' I asked.

'Family,' he said.

I tried to stop them taking my friend but a member of staff punched me in the stomach. Then he grabbed my arm and twisted it behind my back. As he held me, I could see out of the window.

My friend was thrown into the back of a blue-and-white social services van. It drove off into the distance.

I was shocked and I really missed my best friend. Soon after that, in September 1974, I started secondary school.

The children's home was in a posh area of Surrey. Most of the kids who went there were middle class. I could not believe that they did not get beaten by their mums and dads like I did at the care home. I thought they were the ones who were not normal.

Kids can be cruel with name-calling and insults. I would hear the usual names: nigger, sambo, nig-nog, coon-flakes and all that. I gave as good as I got.

One day, one kid said to me, 'At least I got a mum!'

I lost it big time. I punched him in the face.

I got suspended.

In all, I was expelled three times from three secondary schools.

When I was fourteen, a racist kid at school did a 'Planet of the Apes' impersonation of me. I sat at my desk boiling with anger. I planned to get him later.

At lunchtime, I waited in the boys' toilet. I cracked his head against the toilet bowl. I beat him up bad.

The police were called. There was an ambulance.

That night there was a case meeting. It went on for hours. I wasn't even allowed to hear what they were saying about me.

When they had finished, my social worker looked at me. He shook his head.

'You're being moved,' he said. 'To Brixton. Where your parents used to live.'

'Brixton?' I said. 'Where's that?'

'Where your parents used to live,' he said again.

I had to move that same night. I didn't even get to say goodbye to my friends.

What do you think?

- How do you imagine Alex felt when his friend was taken away?

- Alex and his friend were not 'next of kin', but were they 'family'? What makes a family?

- What are the best ways to deal with name-calling and insults?

3

The Frontline

As I was driven away from the care home towards Brixton, I started staring out of the window. I saw a strange thing. Black people! There were grown-up black people. They were just walking along the streets.

It freaked me out. I thought that any black man could have been my dad and any black woman could have been my mum. I wanted to get out of the car.

I was taken to a social services hostel at Elm Park, just off Brixton Hill. It was opposite Brixton prison.

My social worker and the guy who was in charge of the hostel showed me around. I had a small bedroom on the first floor. They gave me a tiny black and white TV that didn't even work.

The guy in charge told me all the rules: 'On Mondays, you will help with the cooking.
On Tuesdays, it's your turn to wash up. On Wednesdays, blah blah blah. On Thursdays, blah blah blah.'

I switched off. What fourteen-year-old wants to hear that stuff?

The guy went on for ages. The last thing he told me was not to go to the Frontline.

'The Frontline?' I said. 'Where is that?'

'It's a street where all the bad people hang out,' he said. 'It's not a place for you. Keep well clear.'

When they finally left me, it was close to midnight. There was only one thing on my mind.

I got out of the hostel by climbing out of my bedroom window. I asked people I met on the street where the Frontline was. They gave me some strange looks because of my Surrey accent. They told me the way to go but I couldn't understand them! The people speaking to me spoke Jamaican English and it was different from anything I had ever heard. I felt really bad, because if I did ever find my mum and dad I wouldn't be able to understand what they were saying.

Anyway, I finally found the Frontline, the area around Railton Road.

The first thing that hit me was the booming noise. There was a deep rumble that sounded like a mini earthquake to my ears. It was coming out of most of the houses. It scared me.

I asked people what the sound was.

'It's the bassline,' was the answer. 'Reggae music!'

On the Frontline, I saw drug dealers, pimps, whores, gangsters, sweet boys and roughnecks. People were just hanging around.

I saw one boy standing on a corner. He looked even younger than me. He was wearing a waistcoat, football shorts and expensive trainers. He looked about twelve.

I went up to him.

'What are you doing out so late?' I asked.

'Move from me, boy!' he said. 'Can't you see I'm trying to sell some weed?'

'Man!' I thought. 'This is Brixton!'

I was hooked. From then on, I was always on the Frontline. There was no way I was going to sit at the hostel and wait in for a teacher to give me my lessons!

What do you think?

- Why was Alex so surprised to see other black people?

- How do you imagine Alex felt when he was sent away from the children's home to live in a hostel?

- Why do you think Alex was hooked on the Frontline?

4
Riot

One afternoon when I was watching the comings and goings on Railton Road, I was recruited.

The man who recruited me was the local crime lord. He wore a cashmere coat, silk shirt, a beaver-skin cowboy hat and crocodile-skin shoes. He had big gold rings on his fingers. He had ruby and gold teeth. He had a bad man's walk. He was the coolest guy I had ever seen.

He bought me a chicken patty and then he asked if I could run fast.

'Of course,' I said.

So he tested me out.

'Do you want to earn some money?' he asked me after I had shown him how fast I could run.

'Of course,' I said.

My job for this crime lord was to be a look-out. I waited outside the house that the crime lord worked from. If I saw any police coming, I would run into the basement shouting, 'Beast, beast, beast.'

He would give me this old brown briefcase. It was part of my job to outrun the police over back gardens and fences and through alleyways. I had to take the briefcase to a safe flat. I was paid around £2 per day. If I did my job well, the crime lord would buy me a chicken patty as a bonus. Man! I loved chicken patties.

After a few weeks, I was asked to sell weed. I would go to all-night blues dances, Brixton pyjama parties, youth clubs and anywhere else where people smoked dope.

In the town halls around Brixton, I would sell weed and hot-step to reggae music from the likes of Dennis Brown, Sugar Minott and Gregory Isaacs.

I got robbed quite a few times and beaten up. But I didn't care. Somebody wanted me. Somebody wanted to pay me.

I was eighteen and still hustling weed when the Brixton Uprising broke out in April 1981.

On the Friday night, I was shooting pool in a pub on Brixton Hill. This young black guy ran in and shouted that the police had stabbed a black youth to death in broad daylight!

We went from house to house, road to road and estate to estate telling everyone the news. It went around Brixton like wildfire.

None of us went to sleep that night. We were all thinking about what might happen tomorrow.

The next day we all set off for central Brixton. We did not know what to expect from the police but we would not take any more abuse from them.

Even though there were a lot of us on the streets, the police tried to arrest a minicab driver nicknamed Wadada. There were more of us than there were police. Before I knew it, a police van was rocked over and its windows were kicked in.

For three days and nights, Brixton burned.

On the first and second days, I spent most of my time fighting the police. They had arrested me and beaten me up a number of times before.

This was a good chance for me to get my revenge. It was amazing to see the police running from us!

On the third day, all of us walked to the centre of Brixton and stood in front of the police wearing the clothes we had looted. It was like being in a dream.

What do you think?

- Alex writes that he didn't care if he got beaten up, because 'somebody wanted me'. What do you think he means by this?

- How easy do you think it is for children like Alex to fall into a life of crime? What other choices do they have?

- Have you ever taken revenge on someone? How did it make you feel? Would you do the same again? Why or why not?

5
Locked up

A few weeks later, I was relaxing at the hostel, playing dominoes with my friends.

One of my mates heard screeching tyres. He looked out of the window and yelled, 'Police!'

Four police vans pulled up outside and about ten policemen got out.

I was soon arrested.

Friends told me, 'Alex, don't tell them anything!'

The police threw me in a van and beat me up. They took me to Brixton police station, gave me another whipping and let me fret in a cell for a few hours.

Then they came back to question me.

One of them said, 'We have reason to believe you have been involved with causing an affray, resisting arrest and assaulting police officers.'

'It wasn't me,' I said. 'I'm a good boy. I'm a Christian.'

They let me fret in the cell again for another couple of hours. Then they returned with a slim brown envelope. They placed it on the table.

I was asked, 'Are you still denying the charges against you?'

'Wasn't me,' I said. 'Believe me! I go to church.'

They took a large photo out of the envelope. It was a full-length picture of me throwing a brick at the police.

I was screwed. I received a ten-month sentence.

I was sent to Wormwood Scrubs.

When I got there, they pushed me into a basement cell. The smell of crap hit me.

Lying down on the top bunk was a man about fifty years old. He had long, greying dreadlocks and a crooked grin. One of his eyes was almost closed and he had only a few teeth. He really scared me. And the smell of his waste coming from a bucket was disgusting. The dread had the runs. Trust my luck!

Lying on my bunk, with the smell of crap filling my nostrils, I thought, 'Who's there for me?'

When I was in the dock, I had thought, 'Where's my mum? Where's my dad?'

I didn't even have an aunt or uncle to help me. I felt like taking my own life. I wanted to end it all. I tried to think of a way I could kill myself without any pain.

In the middle of the night, the dread got out his tatty Bible and started to chant.

'By the rivers of Babylon,' he sang. 'Rastafari! Where we sat down. King of kings! And where we wept. Jah Man! When we remember Zion. Selassie I!'

I could not believe it. The smell of crap was bad enough but the chanting really freaked me out.

What do you think?

- Do you think Alex was telling the truth when he said, 'I'm a good boy'? Why or why not?

- How did the police treat Alex when he was arrested?

- Who is there for you? Are you there for anyone?

6
Education

The dread's chanting went on night after night. It was driving me mad.

After eight nights, I said to myself, 'If he starts chanting again, he won't survive the night. I'm going to mash him up bad.'

He was much older and skinnier than me so I thought it would be no contest.

I lay down on my bunk. The bucket still stank of crap. But I did manage to get to sleep.

Then I was woken by the dread's chanting.

'Daniel in the lions' den and him never get burn!' he sang.

I flipped. I jumped down from my bunk and we went to war.

Ten minutes later I was broken up. How could I know that the dread knew karate? My nostril was split, my bottom lip had tripled its size and my left eye was mangled. I was bleeding from so many places.

I sat in the corner of the cell crying like a girl. The dread was walking up and down, stroking his beard.

'Don't mess with the dread,' he said. 'Rastafari!'

I wanted the screws to help me so I screamed louder. I heard footsteps coming near but the wardens walked right past.

After a while, I think the dread felt sorry for me. He sat down beside me.

'What's wrong with you?' he asked. 'Why do you want to fight me?'

'What's wrong with me?' I said. 'You beat me up! Your chanting is driving me mad! And you do it every night! And your crap stinks.'

'Don't get all worked up again,' he said, slapping me on my head.

That night I ended up telling the dread my whole story.

The dread twisted his beard and said, 'You had it rough, man. Rough inna Babylon! Did you finish school?'

'No,' I said.

He slapped me around the head again.

'You need an education, man!' he told me.

That same morning, after breakfast, the dread took me to the prison library. He got out a book for me to read. It was called *The Black Jacobins* and it was by C. L. R. James. It was about slaves in Haiti who had fought for freedom from their French rulers. I found it exciting and inspiring. Nobody told me this kind of history in school.

For the rest of my prison days, I read and read. Getting my education, as the dread would say.

By the time I left, the dread made me promise him something. He made me promise that I would continue my reading when I got out of prison.

'But I haven't got any money to buy books,' I said.

'Go to your local library,' he said. 'Books are free there.'

Two days after getting out of prison, I went to Brixton library with a black bin bag. I did what the dread had told me. I took out about twenty-five books and put them in my bin bag. As I stepped out of the library, I looked like a black Father Christmas.

What do you think?

- Why did Alex try to beat up the dread? What else could he have done?

- Why do you think the dread told Alex, 'You need an education'? How might an education make a difference to Alex?

- What inspires you?

7

Just a joker?

It was good to be on the Frontline and hear that bassline and reggae again.

I saw that the guys who were involved in the mobile disco business had all the fit girls. The brothers from the top discos drove nice cars and wore beaver-skin hats. I so wanted a beaver-skin hat!

So I got involved with some mates who were building a disco set.

We had no money to buy all the gear that we needed so at night we raided wood yards for sheets of plywood and chipboard. There was a loudspeaker warehouse in Thornton Heath and we burgled that.

We built the speaker boxes ourselves and put our dole money together to buy reggae music. We made sure we had speakers that could give us a thumping bassline.

We arranged to play at our first dance. We didn't have any twin decks so there was a gap when a tune finished. To keep the crowd entertained while we were picking the next vinyl, we needed a man on a microphone.

No one wanted to do it. We decided that whoever pulled the lowest card would be the DJ. I pulled the two of clubs.

My brothers told me to write some lyrics. I didn't bother. I thought I could wing it. Our first dance was a packed party. Ravers were swaying, drinks were flowing and weed was puffing. One of my brothers handed me the microphone.

'Entertain the crowd, man,' he said.

I took a long look at the ravers and I froze. There were so many faces. They were all looking at me, waiting for me to say something. My hands and legs were shaking.

To relieve my nerves, I did this crazy dance. The crowd wondered what I was doing.

I hadn't written any lyrics down so I had to make something up there and then.

'Reggae music, you know!' I cried. 'Dennis Brown! Bob Marley!'

I carried on doing my little dance. Some girls were laughing. Guys were cracking up. Someone shouted, 'Who is this joker?'

Everyone laughed.

I had to put the microphone down and leave. I was so ashamed.

The next day I went down to Brixton market to buy myself a chicken patty. I saw some girls who were at the dance the night before. They saw me. They pointed at me and started giggling the way girls do. I felt crushed.

What did I do? I went to a nearby shop. I was broke so I sort of borrowed a notepad and a few pencils. Security guards could never catch me.

In that notepad, I began my journey as a writer.

What do you think?

- How do you imagine Alex's friends felt when they realized he hadn't planned what to say between records?

- What makes a good team player?

- What do you think is the best way to deal with feeling really embarrassed?

8
Mr DJ

There was this girl. She was about sixteen years old and she was a neighbour of mine. She had this strict church father and he hated his daughter chatting to us roughnecks in the hostel.

One Sunday afternoon, I heard a noise coming from the girl's house. Her father was throwing her out of the house because she was pregnant.

'Come out!' he roared. 'You dirty bitch! Come out!'

He was throwing all her clothes out on to the street.

The girl was screaming, 'No, Daddy! No!'

I went to get my pencil and notepad and I sat on my front steps writing some new lyrics. They went like this:

> How she belly get fat? How she belly get fat?
> It must be the church boy round the corner
>   do that.
> Her daddy going kill him like he's a dirty rat.
> Him a love rat, love rat.

I tried out these lyrics at the next dance. The crowd still thought I was rubbish but at least I was trying. It was a start.

I used to walk around with my notepad and pencil all the time. I worked very hard on my lyrics whenever I could.

I wrote about the things I saw around me and about everyday life in Brixton. I wrote about being poor. I wrote about being unemployed. I wrote about how the police treated young black people in Brixton. Bit by bit I got better.

After a while, people began to like what I had to say and I often got work as a DJ. Sometimes they would ask me to repeat a lyric or song. They used to raise their fists as I performed. I was best known for my Uprising chant.

It went like this:

> Uprising this is an uprising
> Uprising this is an uprising
> Uprising this is an uprising!
> We're sick and tired of the ghetto housing
> And the damn sus law and police beating.
> We have no work and we have no shilling
> We can't take no more of this suffering.

You'd better send for the army and the
   Home Guard
We're gonna mash up and burn down
   New Scotland Yard!
Come listen people to the Brixton bard
Police officer you'd better put up your
   guard!

In those days, I used to wear my army trousers,
Che Guevara T-shirt and black beret. So that the
beret looked round and neat I would bend a coat
hanger in a circle and put it inside. And of course
I had my Brixton strut. I looked rough but cool,
so they called me Yardman Irie.

What do you think?

- What does 'Uprising' say about how Alex felt towards the police and those in authority? Why do you think he felt that way?

- In what ways can people protest against authority? What ways are the most likely to work?

- What could you work hard at? What might happen if you got really good at it?

- If you were a DJ, what would you call yourself and why?

9

Reunion

I worked as a DJ for around four years. Then the poetry jam explosion began. This was when bars opened up for free microphone sessions and spoken-word events. Once a month, if you fancied yourself as a singer, a poet or a comedian – or if you wanted to get things off your chest – you could get up on a small stage and do your thing.

I decided to have a go at saying some of the poems I had written. Trust me, I was nervous.

Saying a poem in front of people sitting down sipping fancy coffee was much harder than being a DJ. I was used to the music and noise of a swaying crowd. It took me a long while to get used to it. But I did OK.

One day, when I was in the middle of a jam, I looked up. At the back of the crowd, there he was. It was my friend from the Surrey children's home. The last time I had seen him was when he was dragged out of our bedroom in the middle of the night and driven away in a van. I could not believe it.

I was so shocked I dropped the microphone. I stopped my act and went to see my brother. Man! It was good to see him.

We caught up on old times. He told me that after he had been taken away he was sent to another children's home in Kent. He did not make any friends there.

When he left care, he stayed in Kent doing handyman work and painting and decorating. But he felt very lonely.

After a few years, he came back to south London to see if he could find any of his old friends. He saw a flyer about a poetry jam with my name on it and decided to check it out.

Things were going well for my friend. He had a good job and a flat. And he had just met a beautiful girl.

We both talked about our lives. We kept in touch and we became best mates again.

About two months later, I got a phone call from my friend. He just called out my name and then the phone went dead. Something was very wrong.

So I ran round to his flat. He lived up on the fourth floor. When I got there, I found that his front door was hanging off its hinges.

The lock was broken. It seemed like someone had gone crazy with a hammer on the door. I pushed my way in. I walked through the hallway and there were hammer marks there too.

All kinds of things were going through my mind. I was worried my friend had been attacked or even killed.

I stepped into the kitchen. The fridge was lying on its side. Milk, eggs and other bits of food were on the floor. Hammer marks were on the walls. The windows were smashed.

I rushed into the lounge. The windows were smashed in here too. The curtains were torn. The coffee table that my friend had built was in pieces. The TV had been kicked in.

I was getting scared now.

I quickly ran into the spare bedroom. He had just started to decorate it. There were pots of paint in one corner. My friend was in another corner. He was crouched down. His head was in his hands. He was rocking backwards and forwards.

What do you think?

- How do you imagine Alex felt when he saw his friend in the crowd? How do you imagine he felt when he saw his friend crouched in the corner of his spare room?

- If you had to put on an act, what would you do? Sing, dance, tell jokes or say a poem? How would you feel about it?

- What are some good ways of dealing with being nervous?

10
Finding my talent

I looked at my friend crouched in the corner of his spare room. I knew something really bad must have happened.

'What happened?' I asked.

'Move from me, man! I can't take this crap!' he said. 'Can't take it any more!'

'Can't take what?' I asked.

'Just get out, man!' He was starting to shout now. 'I can't take it any more. This frigging life!'

I tried again. 'What do you mean?'

'I can't tell you!' he cried. 'Just get out! Leave me alone!'

He went quiet and hid his head behind his hands again.

'I thought we were best mates,' I said. 'Thought we could tell each other anything.'

'Can't tell you this,' he said.

'Can't tell me what?' I shouted. I was getting really frustrated.

'It's my girl,' he said after a while.

'What? You mashed up your flat over a girl? Are you crazy? What's the matter with you? There's plenty of girls out there. Don't worry yourself about this one.'

'You don't understand,' he said.

'What don't I understand?' I screamed.

'The girl is my sister!' he screamed back.

After he had calmed down a bit, he told me what had happened.

He and his girl were getting close. She invited him over for Sunday dinner at her mum's flat.

Her father had gone missing a long time ago but he would turn up now and again, looking for money or food. He turned up when my friend was there. He looked at my friend and thought perhaps he knew him from somewhere.

After my friend's girl and her mother had gone out to wash the pots and dishes, her dad asked my friend for his full name.

My friend told him.

Her dad then asked for my friend's date of birth. My friend told him that too.

The man rocked back into his seat and placed his hands on his head.

'Jesus Christ!' he said. 'You're one of my children!'

My friend ran out. He kept running all the way back to his flat. He was so upset, he smashed it up. He never wanted to go outside again because he thought people were laughing at him.

I didn't know what to do, except to start writing.

I decided to write a story based on my friend's life and on my own. I called it *Brixton Rock*.

My best mate did get over the shock of dating his half-sister. He found a new girl. He is now the happy father of a son and a daughter.

Like me, he wants to be a good dad. We don't want our kids to grow up without dads like we did.

In March 1999, five years after beginning to write it, *Brixton Rock* was published as a book. I was an author and it felt good.

Just to make sure it was all really happening, I went to one of the top bookshops on Oxford Street in central London. And in the 'W' section there it was. There were five copies of *Brixton Rock*!

But you could only see the spines of the books. So I pushed away the books nearby and I turned my book out so that you could see the picture of young black people on the front cover. People needed to see it. People needed to see us.

After *Brixton Rock*, I carried on writing and I had more books published. Many of them are about life in Brixton.

In 2008, the Queen made me a Member of the British Empire for my work in literature. She gave me a medal.

I am now Alex Wheatle MBE. My Brixton friends say I am a Member of the 'Brixton' Empire! This is my story and it is all true. Thank you for reading it.

What do you think?

- How could you help a friend who is going through a really tough time?

- What makes a good dad?

- What do you think Alex means when he writes, 'People needed to see it. People needed to see us'?

Books available in the Diamond series

Space Ark
by Rob Childs (ISBN: 978 1 908713 11 7)
Ben and his family are walking in the woods when they are thrown to the ground by a dazzling light. Ben wakes up to find they have been abducted by aliens. Will Ben be able to defeat the aliens and save his family before it is too late?

Snake
by Matt Dickinson (ISBN: 978 1 908713 12 4)
Liam loves visiting the local pet shop and is desperate to have his own pet snake. Then one day, Mr Nash, the owner of the shop, just disappears. What has happened to Mr Nash? And how far will Liam go to get what he wants?

Fans
by Niall Griffiths (ISBN: 978 1 908713 13 1)
Jerry is excited about taking his young son Stevie to watch the big match. But when trouble breaks out between the fans, Jerry and Stevie can't escape the shouting, fighting and flying glass. And then Stevie gets lost in the crowd. What will Jerry do next? And what will happen to Stevie?

Breaking the Chain

by Darren Richards (ISBN: 978 1 908713 08 7)

Ken had a happy life. But then he found out a secret that changed everything. Now he is in prison for murder. Then Ken meets the new lad on the wing, Josh. Why does Ken tell Josh his secret? And could it be the key to their freedom?

Lost at Sea

by Joel Smith (ISBN: 978 1 908713 09 4)

Alec loves his job in the Royal Navy. His new mission is to save refugees from unsafe boats. But when a daring rescue attempt goes wrong, Alec is the one who needs saving. Who will come to help him?

Uprising: A true story

by Alex Wheatle (ISBN 978 1 908713 10 0)

Alex had a tough start in life. He grew up in care until he was fourteen, when he was sent to live in a hostel in Brixton. After being sent to prison for taking part in the Brixton riots, Alex's future seemed hopeless. But then something happened to change his life…

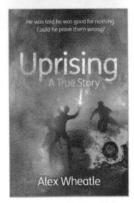

You can order these books by writing to Diffusion, SPCK, 36 Causton Street, London SW1P 4ST or visiting www.spck.org.uk/what-we-do/prison-fiction/